COMPOST!

GROWING GARDENS FROM YOUR GARBAGE

BY LINDA GLASER
PICTURES BY ANCA HARITON

The Millbrook Press
Brookfield, Connecticut

TO JOHN, MY COMPOSTING PARTNER YEAR IN AND
YEAR OUT, SUMMER AND WINTER, RAIN AND SHINE.

LG

TO FARMERS IN EVERY TIME AND FARMERS
EVERYWHERE FROM AVRAM TO ZAMFIRA: IT IS YOUR
LOVE OF EARTH THAT FIRST NOURISHED US.

AH

Library of Congress Cataloging-in-Publication Data
Glaser, Linda
Compost! Grow gardens from your garbage / by Linda
Glaser; pictures by Anca Hariton.
p. cm.
Summary: Aimed at the very young child, this picture
book describes what composting is, what it does, and
how to go about it.
ISBN 1-56294-659-5 (lib.bdg.) ISBN 0-7613-0030-9 (tr.)
1.Compost—Juvenile literature. [1.Compost.] I.Hariton,
Anca, ill. II. Title.
S661.G58 1996
635'.048975—dc20   95-10421   CIP

Published by The Millbrook Press
2 Old New Milford Road, Brookfield, Connecticut 06804

At my house, we grow
          sunflowers, sweet peas, strawberries,
          potatoes, petunias, pansies,
          corn, carrots, cucumbers.

And we use garbage to do it!

This is where it starts—
in our compost bin.
It's just a big box.
But amazing things happen here.

First we throw in the garbage.

Here go
the banana peels from breakfast,
my bread crusts from lunch,
and the carrot scrapings
and apple cores from snack.

I also throw in my lima beans from dinner.
My mom says she wishes I'd eat them.

But I tell her, "I'm not wasting.
I'm composting!"

Here's the moldy jack-o'-lantern
that we carved for Halloween.

It doesn't look like much anymore.
But it's still good for something.
It's good for the compost.
So I dump it in.

We toss in grass clippings and fallen leaves from our yard,

old chopped up cucumber

vines from the garden,

and all our wilted flowers— daisies, dahlias, pansies,

and petunias.   Layer after layer.

Leftovers from our plates
and leftovers from our garden
all end up in our compost bin.

I dump in Lopsy's bunny droppings, too.
So even my rabbit adds to our compost!

Sometimes I hose the pile with water to keep it nice and moist.

Every few weeks,
my mom takes her pitchfork
and tosses the whole pile.

You can feel something happening.
If you hold your hand here,
you can feel the heat.
Sometimes you can even see steam.

That's when you know the garbage is changing. It's called decay. That's nature's way of recycling.

Amazing!
The compost doesn't even
smell like garbage.
It smells fresh like earth.
And it doesn't look like garbage.
It looks like dark brown soil.

Now it's ready to
go into our garden.

We fill the wheelbarrow
and spread the compost all around.
Then we mix and dig, mix and dig.

Now we plant
    sunflowers, sweet peas, strawberries,
    potatoes, petunias, pansies,
    corn, carrots, and cucumbers.

Compost makes the earth rich.
It helps our garden grow
and grow
...and grow!

So that's how composting works.
It keeps on going around and
around from garbage to compost
to garden again and again
and again.

QUESTIONS AND ANSWERS ABOUT COMPOSTING

For adults who might want to start composting with children, here are the answers to some questions they might have.

WHAT'S THE EASIEST WAY TO MAKE COMPOST?

Pile dry fallen leaves and grass clippings in a corner of your backyard. Layer it—leaves and grass, leaves and grass, leaves and grass, using more leaves than grass. Simply let the pile set. Slowly it will become compost all by itself.

HOW DO YOU START A COMPOST BIN?

Some hardware stores sell compost bins. Or you can get a large wooden bin that measures about 30 inches (76 centimeters) wide by 30 inches deep by 30 inches high or just get some chicken wire to form a round "container" of about 30 inches in diameter and 35 inches (90 centimeters) in height. Then dump in your fallen leaves, grass clippings, and kitchen scraps. Mix them all together well. Slowly, they will form compost.

If you want to make compost more quickly, you need to "turn" the compost. Often, two bins are used for turning compost. (There can also be a third bin for storing the compost that is ready to be spread on the garden.)

WHAT CAN GO INTO THE COMPOST?

Anything that comes from a plant or a tree can go into the compost. This type of "garbage" is called "organic matter." If it's big like branches or vines, or thick like orange peels, you should chop it into smaller pieces to help it start breaking down. An adult should supervise the chopping. Plus, animal manure from rabbits and chickens can be added to enrich the compost too. Don't put in meat scraps or dairy products. They attract animals.

CAN YOU MAKE COMPOST IF YOU DON'T HAVE A BACKYARD?

Some cities have composting programs. They collect yard debris and then compost it in big city piles. When it's composted, they let people take it to use in their gardens. Some schools have composting programs. They put leftovers from the cafeteria and leaves from the yard into the compost bin. Or they use a worm composting box indoors. Then they use the compost in a school garden.

WHAT MAKES THE GARBAGE TURN INTO COMPOST?

In the compost bin, tiny bacteria start breaking down the organic matter. Then fungi and protozoans join the bacteria in this breaking-down process. Later, centipedes, millipedes, beetles, and earthworms help, too. This process of breaking down is called "decay" or "decomposition."

Try this simple experiment to see how composting works:

- Fill a large plant pot about 1/3 full of dirt.
- Chop up a few food scraps (an apple core, carrot scrapings, salad—no meat or dairy) and add them to the dirt in the pot.
- Add some more dirt to the pot.
- Turn the mixture with a spoon every few days and keep it damp (not wet) by spraying or sprinkling with water. Always make sure that there is dirt on the top layer after you've turned the mixture over.

Eventually the food scraps will "disappear." They've turned into compost. Now you can plant something in it!

WHY IS COMPOSTING IMPORTANT?

Much garbage thrown away each year is "organic matter," which can be composted. The more we compost, the less garbage we'll have. Plus, compost is valuable. It puts important nutrients back into the soil. It makes the earth richer and helps plants grow. So composting helps the earth in many ways.